NoteBook No. _____	Start Da

MW00955713

This Book Belong To:

Name:	
Address:	
Phone:	
Email:	

As a Reward: $

ISBN-13: 978-1983587818

ISBN-10: 1983587818

Customer Number #: _____

Customer's Name: [ ] Birthday: [ ]

Email: [ ] Phone: [ ]

Occupation: [ ] Notes: [ ]

Address: [ ]

[ ]

Date/Time	Activity	Amount	Comments

Customer Number #: _____

Customer's Name: [   ] Birthday: [   ]

Email: [   ] Phone: [   ]

Occupation: [   ] Notes: [   ]

Address: [   ]

[   ]

Date/Time	Activity	Amount	Comments

Customer Number #: _____

Customer's Name: [　　　　　　　　　] Birthday: [　　]

Email: [　　　　　　　] Phone: [　　　　　　　]

Occupation: [　　　　　　] Notes: [　　　　　　]

Address: [　　　　　　　　　　　　　　　]

[　　　　　　　　　　　　　　　　　　　]

Date/Time	Activity	Amount	Comments

Customer Number #: _____

Customer's Name: [_____] Birthday: [_____]

Email: [_____] Phone: [_____]

Occupation: [_____] Notes: [_____]

Address: [_____]

[_____]

Date/Time	Activity	Amount	Comments

Customer Number #: _____

Customer's Name: [   ] Birthday: [   ]

Email: [   ] Phone: [   ]

Occupation: [   ] Notes: [   ]

Address: [   ]

[   ]

Date/Time	Activity	Amount	Comments

Customer Number #: _____

Customer's Name: [   ] Birthday: [   ]

Email: [   ] Phone: [   ]

Occupation: [   ] Notes: [   ]

Address: [   ]

[   ]

Date/Time	Activity	Amount	Comments

Customer Number #: _____

Customer's Name: _____ Birthday: _____

Email: _____ Phone: _____

Occupation: _____ Notes: _____

Address: _____

_____

Date/Time	Activity	Amount	Comments

Customer Number #: _____

Customer's Name: [   ] Birthday: [   ]

Email: [   ]   Phone: [   ]

Occupation: [   ] Notes: [   ]

Address: [   ]

[   ]

Date/Time	Activity	Amount	Comments

Customer Number #: _____

Customer's Name: [   ] Birthday: [   ]

Email: [   ] Phone: [   ]

Occupation: [   ] Notes: [   ]

Address: [   ]

[   ]

Date/Time	Activity	Amount	Comments

Customer Number #: _____

Customer's Name: [_____] Birthday: [_____]

Email: [_____] Phone: [_____]

Occupation: [_____] Notes: [_____]

Address: [_____]

[_____]

Date/Time	Activity	Amount	Comments

Customer Number #: _____

Customer's Name: [　　　　　　　　　　] Birthday: [　　]

Email: [　　　　　　　] Phone: [　　　　　　]

Occupation: [　　　　　] Notes: [　　　　　　]

Address: [　　　　　　　　　　　]

[　　　　　　　　　　　　　]

Date/Time	Activity	Amount	Comments

Customer Number #: _____

Customer's Name: [ ] Birthday: [ ]

Email: [ ] Phone: [ ]

Occupation: [ ] Notes: [ ]

Address: [ ]

[ ]

Date/Time	Activity	Amount	Comments

Customer Number #: _____

Customer's Name: [　　　　　　　　　] Birthday: [　　]

Email: [　　　　　　] Phone: [　　　　　　]

Occupation: [　　　　] Notes: [　　　　　]

Address: [　　　　　　　　　　　　　　　]

[　　　　　　　　　　　　　　　　　　]

Date/Time	Activity	Amount	Comments

Customer Number #: _____

Customer's Name: _____ Birthday: _____

Email: _____ Phone: _____

Occupation: _____ Notes: _____

Address: _____

Date/Time	Activity	Amount	Comments

Customer Number #: _____

Customer's Name: (_____) Birthday: (_____)

Email: (_____) Phone: (_____)

Occupation: (_____) Notes: (_____)

Address: (_____)

(_____)

Date/Time	Activity	Amount	Comments

Customer Number #: _____

Customer's Name: [   ] Birthday: [   ]

Email: [   ] Phone: [   ]

Occupation: [   ] Notes: [   ]

Address: [   ]

[   ]

Date/Time	Activity	Amount	Comments

Customer Number #: _____

Customer's Name: [_____] Birthday: [_____]

Email: [_____] Phone: [_____]

Occupation: [_____] Notes: [_____]

Address: [_____]

[_____]

Date/Time	Activity	Amount	Comments

Customer Number #: _____

Customer's Name: [_____] Birthday: [_____]

Email: [_____] Phone: [_____]

Occupation: [_____] Notes: [_____]

Address: [_____]

[_____]

Date/Time	Activity	Amount	Comments

Customer Number #: _____

Customer's Name: _____ Birthday: _____

Email: _____ Phone: _____

Occupation: _____ Notes: _____

Address: _____

_____

Date/Time	Activity	Amount	Comments

Customer Number #: _____

Customer's Name: [_____] Birthday: [_____]

Email: [_____] Phone: [_____]

Occupation: [_____] Notes: [_____]

Address: [_____]

[_____]

Date/Time	Activity	Amount	Comments

Customer Number #: _____

Customer's Name: (_____) Birthday: (_____)

Email: (_____) Phone: (_____)

Occupation: (_____) Notes: (_____)

Address: (_____)

(_____)

Date/Time	Activity	Amount	Comments

Customer Number #: _____

Customer's Name: [   ] Birthday: [   ]

Email: [   ] Phone: [   ]

Occupation: [   ] Notes: [   ]

Address: [   ]

[   ]

Date/Time	Activity	Amount	Comments

Customer Number #: _____

Customer's Name: [   ] Birthday: [   ]

Email: [   ] Phone: [   ]

Occupation: [   ] Notes: [   ]

Address: [   ]

[   ]

Date/Time	Activity	Amount	Comments

Customer Number #: _____

Customer's Name: [ ] Birthday: [ ]

Email: [ ] Phone: [ ]

Occupation: [ ] Notes: [ ]

Address: [ ]

[ ]

Date/Time	Activity	Amount	Comments

Customer Number #: _____

Customer's Name: [_____] Birthday: [_____]

Email: [_____] Phone: [_____]

Occupation: [_____] Notes: [_____]

Address: [_____]

[_____]

Date/Time	Activity	Amount	Comments

Customer Number #: _____

Customer's Name: _____ Birthday: _____

Email: _____ Phone: _____

Occupation: _____ Notes: _____

Address: _____

_____

Date/Time	Activity	Amount	Comments

Customer Number #: _____

Customer's Name: [　　　　　　　] Birthday: [　　　]

Email: [　　　　　　] Phone: [　　　　　　]

Occupation: [　　　　] Notes: [　　　　　]

Address: [　　　　　　　　　　　]

[　　　　　　　　　　　]

Date/Time	Activity	Amount	Comments

Customer Number #: _____

Customer's Name: ( ) Birthday: ( )

Email: ( ) Phone: ( )

Occupation: ( ) Notes: ( )

Address: ( )

( )

Date/Time	Activity	Amount	Comments

Customer Number #: _____

Customer's Name: [   ] Birthday: [   ]

Email: [   ] Phone: [   ]

Occupation: [   ] Notes: [   ]

Address: [   ]

[   ]

Date/Time	Activity	Amount	Comments

Customer Number #: _____

Customer's Name: [   ] Birthday: [   ]

Email: [   ] Phone: [   ]

Occupation: [   ] Notes: [   ]

Address: [   ]

[   ]

Date/Time	Activity	Amount	Comments

Customer Number #: _____

Customer's Name: [   ] Birthday: [   ]

Email: [   ] Phone: [   ]

Occupation: [   ] Notes: [   ]

Address: [   ]

[   ]

Date/Time	Activity	Amount	Comments

Customer Number #: _____

Customer's Name: [_____] Birthday: [_____]

Email: [_____] Phone: [_____]

Occupation: [_____] Notes: [_____]

Address: [_____]

[_____]

Date/Time	Activity	Amount	Comments

Customer Number #: _____

Customer's Name: [_____] Birthday: [____]

Email: [_____] Phone: [_____]

Occupation: [_____] Notes: [_____]

Address: [_____]

[_____]

Date/Time	Activity	Amount	Comments

Customer Number #: _____

Customer's Name: (_____) Birthday: (_____)

Email: (_____) Phone: (_____)

Occupation: (_____) Notes: (_____)

Address: (_____)

(_____)

Date/Time	Activity	Amount	Comments

Customer Number #: _____

Customer's Name: [_____] Birthday: [_____]

Email: [_____] Phone: [_____]

Occupation: [_____] Notes: [_____]

Address: [_____]

[_____]

Date/Time	Activity	Amount	Comments

Customer Number #: _____

Customer's Name: [   ] Birthday: [   ]

Email: [   ] Phone: [   ]

Occupation: [   ] Notes: [   ]

Address: [   ]

[   ]

Date/Time	Activity	Amount	Comments

Customer Number #: _____

Customer's Name: [_____] Birthday: [_____]

Email: [_____] Phone: [_____]

Occupation: [_____] Notes: [_____]

Address: [_____]

[_____]

Date/Time	Activity	Amount	Comments

Customer Number #: _____

Customer's Name: ( ) Birthday: ( )

Email: ( ) Phone: ( )

Occupation: ( ) Notes: ( )

Address: ( )

( )

Date/Time	Activity	Amount	Comments

Customer Number #: _____

Customer's Name: [   ] Birthday: [   ]

Email: [   ] Phone: [   ]

Occupation: [   ] Notes: [   ]

Address: [   ]

[   ]

Date/Time	Activity	Amount	Comments

Customer Number #: _____

Customer's Name: (_____) Birthday: (_____)

Email: (_____) Phone: (_____)

Occupation: (_____) Notes: (_____)

Address: (_____)

(_____)

Date/Time	Activity	Amount	Comments

Customer Number #: _____

Customer's Name: [_____] Birthday: [_____]

Email: [_____] Phone: [_____]

Occupation: [_____] Notes: [_____]

Address: [_____]

[_____]

Date/Time	Activity	Amount	Comments

Customer Number #: _____

Customer's Name: [   ] Birthday: [   ]

Email: [   ] Phone: [   ]

Occupation: [   ] Notes: [   ]

Address: [   ]

[   ]

Date/Time	Activity	Amount	Comments

Customer Number #: _____

Customer's Name: [_____] Birthday: [_____]

Email: [_____] Phone: [_____]

Occupation: [_____] Notes: [_____]

Address: [_____]

[_____]

Date/Time	Activity	Amount	Comments

Customer Number #: _____

Customer's Name: [　　　　　　　　　] Birthday: [　　　　]

Email: [　　　　　　　　] Phone: [　　　　　　　]

Occupation: [　　　　　　] Notes: [　　　　　　　　]

Address: [　　　　　　　　　　　　　　　　　　]

[　　　　　　　　　　　　　　　　　　　　　　]

Date/Time	Activity	Amount	Comments

Customer Number #: _____

Customer's Name: [   ] Birthday: [   ]

Email: [   ] Phone: [   ]

Occupation: [   ] Notes: [   ]

Address: [   ]

[   ]

Date/Time	Activity	Amount	Comments

Customer Number #: _____

Customer's Name: _____ Birthday: _____

Email: _____ Phone: _____

Occupation: _____ Notes: _____

Address: _____

_____

Date/Time	Activity	Amount	Comments

Customer Number #: _____

Customer's Name: [ ] Birthday: [ ]

Email: [ ] Phone: [ ]

Occupation: [ ] Notes: [ ]

Address: [ ]

[ ]

Date/Time	Activity	Amount	Comments

Customer Number #: _____

Customer's Name: [_____] Birthday: [_____]

Email: [_____] Phone: [_____]

Occupation: [_____] Notes: [_____]

Address: [_____]

[_____]

Date/Time	Activity	Amount	Comments

Customer Number #: _____

Customer's Name: [   ] Birthday: [   ]

Email: [   ] Phone: [   ]

Occupation: [   ] Notes: [   ]

Address: [   ]

[   ]

Date/Time	Activity	Amount	Comments

Customer Number #: _____

Customer's Name: [   ] Birthday: [   ]

Email: [   ] Phone: [   ]

Occupation: [   ] Notes: [   ]

Address: [   ]

[   ]

Date/Time	Activity	Amount	Comments

Customer Number #: _____

Customer's Name: ( ) Birthday: ( )

Email: ( ) Phone: ( )

Occupation: ( ) Notes: ( )

Address: ( )

( )

Date/Time	Activity	Amount	Comments

Customer Number #: _____

Customer's Name: (   ) Birthday: (   )

Email: (   ) Phone: (   )

Occupation: (   ) Notes: (   )

Address: (   )

(   )

Date/Time	Activity	Amount	Comments

Customer Number #: _____

Customer's Name: [   ] Birthday: [   ]

Email: [   ] Phone: [   ]

Occupation: [   ] Notes: [   ]

Address: [   ]

[   ]

Date/Time	Activity	Amount	Comments

Customer Number #: _____

Customer's Name: [   ] Birthday: [   ]

Email: [   ] Phone: [   ]

Occupation: [   ] Notes: [   ]

Address: [   ]

[   ]

Date/Time	Activity	Amount	Comments

Customer Number #: _____

Customer's Name: [   ] Birthday: [   ]

Email: [   ] Phone: [   ]

Occupation: [   ] Notes: [   ]

Address: [   ]

[   ]

Date/Time	Activity	Amount	Comments

Customer Number #: _____

Customer's Name: [   ] Birthday: [   ]

Email: [   ] Phone: [   ]

Occupation: [   ] Notes: [   ]

Address: [   ]

[   ]

Date/Time	Activity	Amount	Comments

Customer Number #: _____

Customer's Name: _____ Birthday: _____

Email: _____ Phone: _____

Occupation: _____ Notes: _____

Address: _____

_____

Date/Time	Activity	Amount	Comments

Customer Number #: _____

Customer's Name: [   ] Birthday: [   ]

Email: [   ] Phone: [   ]

Occupation: [   ] Notes: [   ]

Address: [   ]

[   ]

Date/Time	Activity	Amount	Comments

Customer Number #: _____

Customer's Name: [   ] Birthday: [   ]

Email: [   ] Phone: [   ]

Occupation: [   ] Notes: [   ]

Address: [   ]

[   ]

Date/Time	Activity	Amount	Comments

Customer Number #: _____

Customer's Name: [   ] Birthday: [   ]

Email: [   ] Phone: [   ]

Occupation: [   ] Notes: [   ]

Address: [   ]

[   ]

Date/Time	Activity	Amount	Comments

Customer Number #: _____

Customer's Name: [   ] Birthday: [   ]

Email: [   ] Phone: [   ]

Occupation: [   ] Notes: [   ]

Address: [   ]

[   ]

Date/Time	Activity	Amount	Comments

Customer Number #: _____

Customer's Name: ⬭⬭⬭⬭⬭⬭⬭⬭ Birthday: ⬭⬭⬭⬭⬭⬭

Email: ⬭⬭⬭⬭⬭⬭ Phone: ⬭⬭⬭⬭⬭⬭

Occupation: ⬭⬭⬭⬭⬭ Notes: ⬭⬭⬭⬭⬭⬭

Address: ⬭⬭⬭⬭⬭⬭⬭⬭⬭⬭⬭⬭

Date/Time	Activity	Amount	Comments

Customer Number #: _____

Customer's Name: _____ Birthday: _____

Email: _____ Phone: _____

Occupation: _____ Notes: _____

Address: _____

_____

Date/Time	Activity	Amount	Comments

Customer Number #: _____

Customer's Name: [   ] Birthday: [   ]

Email: [   ] Phone: [   ]

Occupation: [   ] Notes: [   ]

Address: [   ]

[   ]

Date/Time	Activity	Amount	Comments

Customer Number #: _____

Customer's Name: [ ] Birthday: [ ]

Email: [ ] Phone: [ ]

Occupation: [ ] Notes: [ ]

Address: [ ]

[ ]

Date/Time	Activity	Amount	Comments

Customer Number #: _____

Customer's Name: [＿＿＿＿＿＿＿＿＿] Birthday: [＿＿＿]

Email: [＿＿＿＿＿＿＿＿] Phone: [＿＿＿＿＿＿＿]

Occupation: [＿＿＿＿＿＿] Notes: [＿＿＿＿＿＿]

Address: [＿＿＿＿＿＿＿＿＿＿＿＿＿＿＿]

[＿＿＿＿＿＿＿＿＿＿＿＿＿＿＿＿＿]

Date/Time	Activity	Amount	Comments

Customer Number #: _____

Customer's Name: [   ]   Birthday: [   ]

Email: [   ]   Phone: [   ]

Occupation: [   ]   Notes: [   ]

Address: [   ]

[   ]

Date/Time	Activity	Amount	Comments

Customer Number #: _____

Customer's Name: [   ] Birthday: [   ]

Email: [   ] Phone: [   ]

Occupation: [   ] Notes: [   ]

Address: [   ]

[   ]

Date/Time	Activity	Amount	Comments

Customer Number #: _____

Customer's Name: [   ] Birthday: [   ]

Email: [   ] Phone: [   ]

Occupation: [   ] Notes: [   ]

Address: [   ]

[   ]

Date/Time	Activity	Amount	Comments

Customer Number #: _____

Customer's Name: [   ] Birthday: [   ]

Email: [   ] Phone: [   ]

Occupation: [   ] Notes: [   ]

Address: [   ]

[   ]

Date/Time	Activity	Amount	Comments

Customer Number #: _____

Customer's Name: [_____] Birthday: [_____]

Email: [_____] Phone: [_____]

Occupation: [_____] Notes: [_____]

Address: [_____]

[_____]

Date/Time	Activity	Amount	Comments

Customer Number #: _____

Customer's Name: [_____] Birthday: [_____]

Email: [_____] Phone: [_____]

Occupation: [_____] Notes: [_____]

Address: [_____]

[_____]

Date/Time	Activity	Amount	Comments

Customer Number #: _____

Customer's Name: ⬭⬭⬭⬭⬭⬭⬭⬭ Birthday: ⬭⬭⬭⬭

Email: ⬭⬭⬭⬭⬭⬭ Phone: ⬭⬭⬭⬭⬭⬭

Occupation: ⬭⬭⬭⬭⬭ Notes: ⬭⬭⬭⬭⬭

Address: ⬭⬭⬭⬭⬭⬭⬭⬭⬭⬭

⬭⬭⬭⬭⬭⬭⬭⬭⬭⬭

Date/Time	Activity	Amount	Comments

Customer Number #: _____

Customer's Name: [   ] Birthday: [   ]

Email: [   ] Phone: [   ]

Occupation: [   ] Notes: [   ]

Address: [   ]

[   ]

Date/Time	Activity	Amount	Comments

Customer Number #: _____

Customer's Name: [   ] Birthday: [   ]

Email: [   ] Phone: [   ]

Occupation: [   ] Notes: [   ]

Address: [   ]

[   ]

Date/Time	Activity	Amount	Comments

Customer Number #: _____

Customer's Name: [ ] Birthday: [ ]

Email: [ ] Phone: [ ]

Occupation: [ ] Notes: [ ]

Address: [ ]

[ ]

Date/Time	Activity	Amount	Comments

Customer Number #: _____

Customer's Name: [   ] Birthday: [   ]

Email: [   ] Phone: [   ]

Occupation: [   ] Notes: [   ]

Address: [   ]

[   ]

Date/Time	Activity	Amount	Comments

Customer Number #: _____

Customer's Name: _____ Birthday: _____

Email: _____ Phone: _____

Occupation: _____ Notes: _____

Address: _____

_____

Date/Time	Activity	Amount	Comments

Customer Number #: _____

Customer's Name: [   ] Birthday: [   ]

Email: [   ] Phone: [   ]

Occupation: [   ] Notes: [   ]

Address: [   ]

[   ]

Date/Time	Activity	Amount	Comments

Customer Number #: _____

Customer's Name: [   ] Birthday: [   ]

Email: [   ] Phone: [   ]

Occupation: [   ] Notes: [   ]

Address: [   ]

[   ]

Date/Time	Activity	Amount	Comments

Customer Number #: _____

Customer's Name: _____ Birthday: _____

Email: _____ Phone: _____

Occupation: _____ Notes: _____

Address: _____

_____

Date/Time	Activity	Amount	Comments

Customer Number #: _____

Customer's Name: _____ Birthday: _____

Email: _____ Phone: _____

Occupation: _____ Notes: _____

Address: _____

_____

Date/Time	Activity	Amount	Comments

Customer Number #: _____

Customer's Name: _____ Birthday: _____

Email: _____ Phone: _____

Occupation: _____ Notes: _____

Address: _____

_____

Date/Time	Activity	Amount	Comments

Customer Number #: _____

Customer's Name: [   ] Birthday: [   ]

Email: [   ] Phone: [   ]

Occupation: [   ] Notes: [   ]

Address: [   ]

[   ]

Date/Time	Activity	Amount	Comments

Customer Number #: _____

Customer's Name: _____ Birthday: _____

Email: _____ Phone: _____

Occupation: _____ Notes: _____

Address: _____

_____

Date/Time	Activity	Amount	Comments

Customer Number #: _____

Customer's Name: [   ] Birthday: [   ]

Email: [   ] Phone: [   ]

Occupation: [   ] Notes: [   ]

Address: [   ]

[   ]

Date/Time	Activity	Amount	Comments

Customer Number #: _____

Customer's Name: _____ Birthday: _____

Email: _____ Phone: _____

Occupation: _____ Notes: _____

Address: _____

_____

Date/Time	Activity	Amount	Comments

Customer Number #: _____

Customer's Name: [   ] Birthday: [   ]

Email: [   ] Phone: [   ]

Occupation: [   ] Notes: [   ]

Address: [   ]

[   ]

Date/Time	Activity	Amount	Comments

Customer Number #: _____

Customer's Name: [＿＿＿＿＿＿＿] Birthday: [＿＿＿]

Email: [＿＿＿＿＿＿] Phone: [＿＿＿＿＿]

Occupation: [＿＿＿＿＿] Notes: [＿＿＿＿＿]

Address: [＿＿＿＿＿＿＿＿＿＿＿]

[＿＿＿＿＿＿＿＿＿＿＿＿＿]

Date/Time	Activity	Amount	Comments

Customer Number #: _____

Customer's Name: (   ) Birthday: (   )

Email: (   )   Phone: (   )

Occupation: (   )   Notes: (   )

Address: (   )

(   )

Date/Time	Activity	Amount	Comments

Customer Number #: _____

Customer's Name: [   ] Birthday: [   ]

Email: [   ] Phone: [   ]

Occupation: [   ] Notes: [   ]

Address: [   ]

[   ]

Date/Time	Activity	Amount	Comments

Customer Number #: _____

Customer's Name: _____ Birthday: _____

Email: _____ Phone: _____

Occupation: _____ Notes: _____

Address: _____

_____

Date/Time	Activity	Amount	Comments

Customer Number #: _____

Customer's Name: _____ Birthday: _____

Email: _____ Phone: _____

Occupation: _____ Notes: _____

Address: _____

_____

Date/Time	Activity	Amount	Comments

Customer Number #: _____

Customer's Name: [   ] Birthday: [   ]

Email: [   ] Phone: [   ]

Occupation: [   ] Notes: [   ]

Address: [   ]

[   ]

Date/Time	Activity	Amount	Comments

Customer Number #: _____

Customer's Name: [   ] Birthday: [   ]

Email: [   ] Phone: [   ]

Occupation: [   ] Notes: [   ]

Address: [   ]

[   ]

Date/Time	Activity	Amount	Comments

Customer Number #: _____

Customer's Name: [_____] Birthday: [_____]

Email: [_____] Phone: [_____]

Occupation: [_____] Notes: [_____]

Address: [_____]

[_____]

Date/Time	Activity	Amount	Comments

Customer Number #: _____

Customer's Name: [   ] Birthday: [   ]

Email: [   ] Phone: [   ]

Occupation: [   ] Notes: [   ]

Address: [   ]

[   ]

Date/Time	Activity	Amount	Comments

Customer Number #: _____

Customer's Name: [   ] Birthday: [   ]

Email: [   ] Phone: [   ]

Occupation: [   ] Notes: [   ]

Address: [   ]

[   ]

Date/Time	Activity	Amount	Comments

Customer Number #: _____

Customer's Name: [_____] Birthday: [____]

Email: [_____] Phone: [_____]

Occupation: [_____] Notes: [_____]

Address: [_____]

[_____]

Date/Time	Activity	Amount	Comments

Customer Number #: _____

Customer's Name: [_____] Birthday: [_____]

Email: [_____] Phone: [_____]

Occupation: [_____] Notes: [_____]

Address: [_____]

[_____]

Date/Time	Activity	Amount	Comments

Customer Number #: _____

Customer's Name: _____ Birthday: _____

Email: _____ Phone: _____

Occupation: _____ Notes: _____

Address: _____

_____

Date/Time	Activity	Amount	Comments

Customer Number #: _____

Customer's Name: _____ Birthday: _____

Email: _____ Phone: _____

Occupation: _____ Notes: _____

Address: _____

_____

Date/Time	Activity	Amount	Comments

Customer Number #: _____

Customer's Name: [   ] Birthday: [   ]

Email: [   ] Phone: [   ]

Occupation: [   ] Notes: [   ]

Address: [   ]

[   ]

Date/Time	Activity	Amount	Comments

Customer Number #: _____

Customer's Name: [   ] Birthday: [   ]

Email: [   ] Phone: [   ]

Occupation: [   ] Notes: [   ]

Address: [   ]

[   ]

Date/Time	Activity	Amount	Comments

Customer Number #: _____

Customer's Name: ( ) Birthday: ( )

Email: ( ) Phone: ( )

Occupation: ( ) Notes: ( )

Address: ( )

( )

Date/Time	Activity	Amount	Comments

Made in the USA
Columbia, SC
22 February 2018